Fortnite Battle Royale Guide

From How to Play to Top Secrets, Hacks and Tricks
To Become A Pro

By Alex Cattington

Copyright

Copyright © 2018. Alex Cattington.

Fortnite Battle Royale Guide From How to Play to Top Secrets, Hacks and Tricks To Become A Pro

Front cover image by Alex Cattington.

Book design by Alex Cattington.

ISBN-13: 978-1718700017

ISBN-10: 1718700016

www.creagear.com

General Overview

History:

Fortnite battle Royale made waves when it was released. The moment it was launched it topped Twitch's chart. From time to on its stats shows to outperform its inspiration player unknown battleground (PUBG). In short, it proved to be a new sensation among gamers.

Fortnite Battle Royale was designed and programmed by Epic games. The free-to-play game is released as an early access to Microsoft windows, macOS, PlayStation 4 and Xbox 1 in September 2017. It was later released for iOS in March 2018 and plans to storm android as well.

The idea of Fortnite Battle Royale came when Fortnite was released mid-2017. The great response on the release of Player Unknown Battleground on March 2017, the game which brought recognition to the Battle Royale genre, Epic Games developer saw an opportunity to enhance the game further by creating a Battle Royale mode out of Fortnite.

Initially, it was launched as a mode within the original gameplay, however, owing to its fame which skyrocketed the original game it was later given independence and was launched as a standalone game. This game is free to play.

If you are reading this e-book it is safe to assume that you have at least played few rounds of PUBG, because if you have, you can easily affiliate with its newer version Battle Royale. However, we will be lying if we say they are clones. There is a very stark difference between the two games, and Battle survivalist should be well aware of them (for the sake of survival!).

The difference does not only lie in the mechanics (which is obvious) but survivalist skills as well. Like we mentioned earlier, it is an enhanced version which requires pro skills. You need to be a master craftsman who is skilled enough to knock up defensive forts in the minimum time possible. A particularly mindboggling point in the game when bold 100 have been destroyed to few ten or so, the best trick in that situation is to use a handful of devious traps which will give a major shock to your opponent.

We are writing this hack book for you which will give you a complete understanding of the game along with various aspects involved to make your gameplay standout. So, whether you're a PUBG pro or complete freshmen to this game, this eBook will be your ultimate guide aiming to make you an elite player.

Synopsis:

Before we start off, it is important to understand the storyline of the game.

One day, almost 98% of earth's population disappears from the land. Those who found themselves still on gravity saw dense clouds, creating chaotic storms that dropped shells, human zombie-like beings, that attacked the living.

The survivors of the destruction innovated ways to build "storm shields", an arena that destroyed the storm clouds from instantly overhead and minimized the attacks from husks. These shields are used to build survivor bases across the globe.

The player is a chief of one of these bases. The mission is to stay in the storm eye and find resources, survivors, and other allies and expand their zones. He is to also find a way to restore the earth to its normal state.

Gameplay:

The gameplay of Fortnite Battle Royale is the same as the standard Battle Royale.

About 100 players are airdropped from a floating party bus. The players land in random places or they can choose a specific place on the map. Every player has a pickaxe by default. They collect weapons and resources as they move on the map.

The end goal of the game is to be the last player, squad or team (depends on how you play) alive by killing other players. As the time passes, the game safe zone which is represented by the eye of the storm starts shrinking. The players outside the safe zone will die as a result of taking potential damage. This scenario forces the players to be in tighter spaces, making them battle each other. Players can also loot equipment from their defeated enemies.

In Fortnite, almost every object can be broken down into resources such as wood, bricks, and steel. They are then used to build forts of limited sustenance, such as stairs, ramps and walls. These objects get more lethal because they can also be used to traverse the map, shield against gunfire or slow down the progress of other players.

The free gameplay is backed by its own microtransactions. It means players can buy V-bucks, specific currency used in the game. The main Fortnite "Save the World" also gives an possibility to earn V-bucks by fulfilling different tasks. The money can be used to enhance players cosmetic appearances such as heroes, characters, weapon skins and emotes.

Another purpose of V-buck is that it helps accelerate the rate that the players advances its tier within the game's season. Each season usually takes few months to complete. By raising their tier, the player automatically gets rewards of cosmetic items for their character which usually revolves around the theme.

Here is a bulleted overview of how the game works. If you are already a survivor and looking for hacks you can skip this section. However, if you are new to the game, don't worry, we got you covered. Here is how it begins:

- Battle Royale was originally built as an extension of Fortnite, a cooperative survival sandbox game from Epic.

- After its rise to fame, it began as a standalone, free gameplay. Refund will be given to those who bought the game in its pre-release form.

- The game is free to play, however, it does come with options for premium editions which will give your special cosmetic items, EXP boosters etc.

- It puts 100 players in a single map and the last man standing wins the game.

- You can play solo, in teams or group (with up to 3 members)

- Location on the map and survivals equipment are randomly distributed. However, you can choose when to jump and the moment you land, looting starts. Your sole purpose at this point is to get as many resources as you can. Killing enemy at this point is also very helpful.

- It's crafting option lets players to gather building resources and build structures whenever push comes to shove. Certain materials are stronger than others and provide more durability.

- Since the winner is the player who outlives everyone. Many among you will choose to hide, to stop that from happening and ensure everyone is equally part of the combat, a mechanic called The Storm Eye, which shrinks the playable area over time. Players who are slow to move new location get caught in the storm quickly and take lethal damage. The idea is to get more players engaged with each other.

How to Start Playing

Requirements

If you are getting started and want to download the game and become a part of the sensation, you have come to the right place. We have got all the information you need to get started.

PC Requirements:

Following are the PC requirements recommended by the Epic games for Fortnite:

Suggested System Requirements for full experience:

- Nvidia GTX 660 or AMD Radeon HD 7870 equivalent DX11 GPU;
- 2 GByte VRAM;
- Core i5 2.8 GHz;
- 8 GB RAM;
- Windows 7/8/10 64-bit.

Lowest System Requirements:

- Intel HD 4000;
- Core i3 2.4 GHz;
- 4 GB RAM;
- Windows 7/8/10 64-bit + Mac OSX Sierra (10.12.6+).

This is good news for gaming PC which has not been upgraded. In other words, PC's that have not been upgraded in over 5 years still fall under the recommended settings. You can also enjoy this game with CPU's own integrated graphics.

Xbox Requirements:

- Available on Xbox One (S, X);
- A stable internet connection;
- Xbox Live Gold required.

PlayStation Requirements:

A stable internet connection with minimum speed 5Mbps is good to go. The lower ping your connection has the better.

- An adult PSN account;
- An accepted payment method;
- A DualShock 4/3 controller.

iOS System Requirements:

- Requires an internet connection and iOS 11;
- Works with: iPhone SE, 6S, 7, 8, X; iPad Mini 4, Air 2, 2017, Pro;
- **Fortnite DOES NOT support: iPhone 5S, 6, 6 Plus; iPad Air, Mini 2, Mini 3, iPod Touch.**

Download size: PS4, Xbox One, and PC/Mac

Given below is the list approximate download size of every system:

- PS4 - 7.471 GB;
- Xbox One - 16.44 GB;
- PC/Mac - 19.76 GB;
- iOS - 130.7 MB.

Note: *As the game keeps on changing with regular updates and fixtures, the numbers will mostly increase as the time goes on. Although, increase in the size may not always be the case, as when the first major map update happened the files size decreased by 2GB's on both PC and PS4. The case can be expected in Xbox as well. Such variations can only be expected through optimized changes that make things run smoothly.*

Installation

PS4:

Go to the PlayStation Store and type for Fortnite Battle Royale. Once found, add it to your basket, confirm 'purchase' (although it is for free) and the download begins. For more accessibility, you can also do it from your PC using the web version of the PlayStation Store.

- On the main manure screen, go to the PlayStation Store.
- Try by typing 'Fort' into the search bar and click when Fortnite: Battle Royale appears in the right suggestion box.
- After landing on the official page just click on the download button.
- To check the download progress, click the notifications icon on the main menu.

Xbox One:

Similar to PS4, you have to search the game in the store. The game should be free to download, those that come with payment are the premium additions to the base game. You can do the same on your browser.

• Navigate the search bar on your homepage and type in "Fortnite".

• Loads of suggestions will appear at the top right box on the screen. Select the one titled 'Fortnite: Battle Royale', not 'Fortnite: Battle Royale Standard' or 'Deluxe'.

• Click install and the game will start downloading.

PC/Mac:

• It is a bit different from the previous two but that does not mean it's hard. The downloading steps are simple to follow.

• Go to the official website of Fortnite:

https://www.epicgames.com/fortnite/en-US/buy-now/battle-royale

• When you reach the page through the link above, click on the bottom left download link.

• Now, you are required to sign in with Epic games through either your email or social media accounts.

• Once you are verified, download the Epic's game launcher.

• Open the launcher, log in to your registered account and search the Fortnite tab.

• Click "install" and enjoy!

Mobile/iOS:

- Just log in App store and download the game.
- It is completely free.

Controls

All pro or intermediate gamers have one thing in common, that is they know the controls of the game like the back of their hand. It is important while playing games to not think about what buttons to go through when playing. Those who fumble, often die before they can figure out the buttons of their combo attacks. This can be a huge setback. While practice makes a man perfect, it won't do you any harm if you go through the controls given here.

Let's began:

PC Controls:

- Up, Down, Left, Right – *WASD;*
- Cursor Mode – *Left Alt/Right Alt;*
- Jump – *SpaceBar;*
- Fire – *Left Mouse Button;*
- Aim Down Sight (ADS) – *Right Mouse Button;*
- Reload – *R;*
- Use – *E;*
- Trap Equip/Picker – *T;*
- Building Edit – *G;*
- Repair/Upgrade – *F;*
- Rotate Building – *R;*
- Sprint – *Left Shift;*
- Change Building Material – *Right Mouse Button;*
- Reset Building Edit – *Right Mouse Button;*

- Weapons Slots – *1, 2, 3, 4;*
- Ability Slots – *5, 6, 7;*
- Gadget Slots – *8, 9;*
- Building Slots – *F1, F2, F3, F4;*
- Trap Slot – *F5;*
- Switch Quickbar – *Q;*
- Slot Up - *Mouse Wheel Down;*
- Slot Down – *Mouse Wheel Down;*
- Chat – *Enter;*
- Quick Chat Message – *B;*
- Place a Note – *N;*
- Spot Target - *Middle Mouse Button;*
- Selected Building Type – *V;*
- Toggle Map – *M;*
- Toggle Inventory – *I;*
- Skip Cutscene – *SpaceBar;*
- Resurrect - *Left Mouse Button;*
- Respawn - *Right Mouse Button;*
- Crouch - *Left Ctrl;*
- Push to Talk – *Y;*

For faster building, we suggest that you rebind 'Building Option 2' and 'Building Option 3' to *F* and *V*, respectively or you can choose the keys you are comfortable using.

PS4 Controls:

- Combat

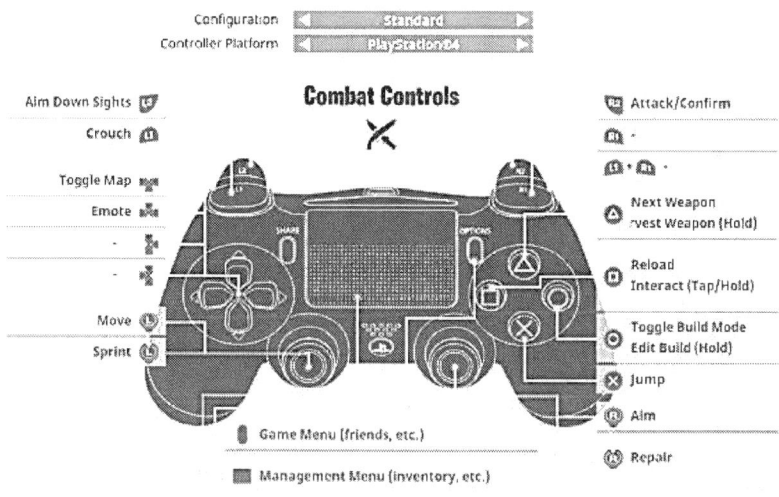

- Building

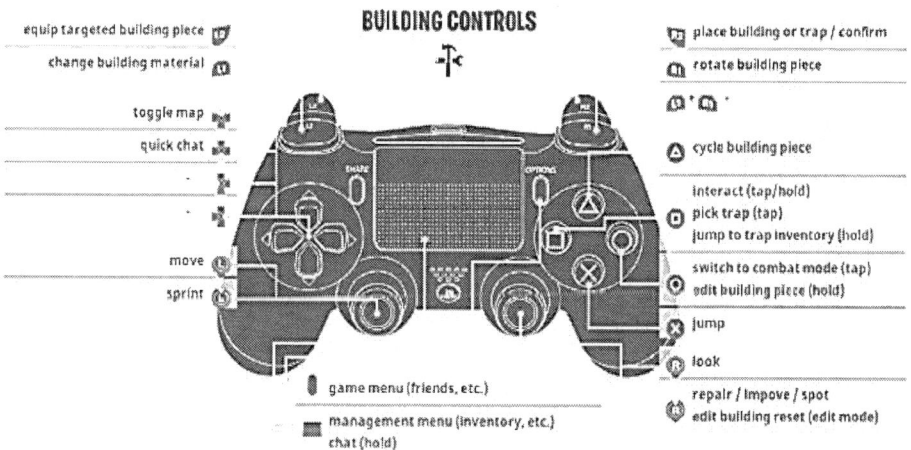

Xbox Controls:

- ## Combat

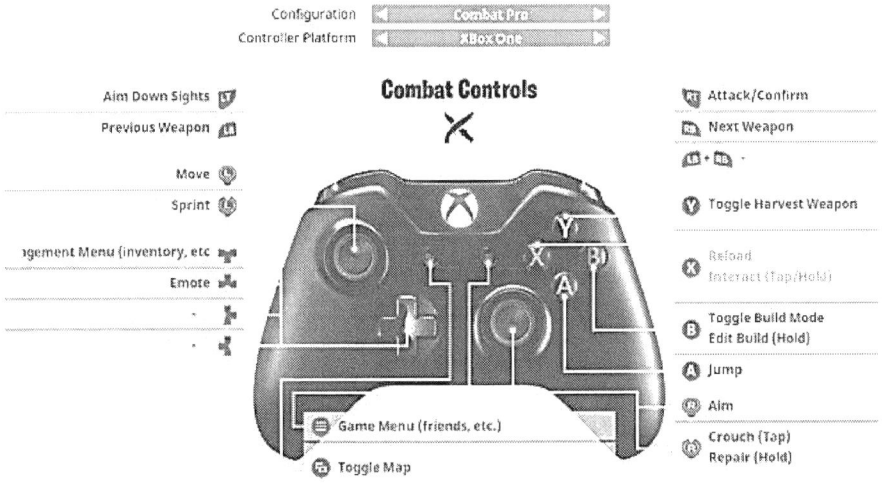

- ## Building

Mobile/iOS:

- Combat

- Building

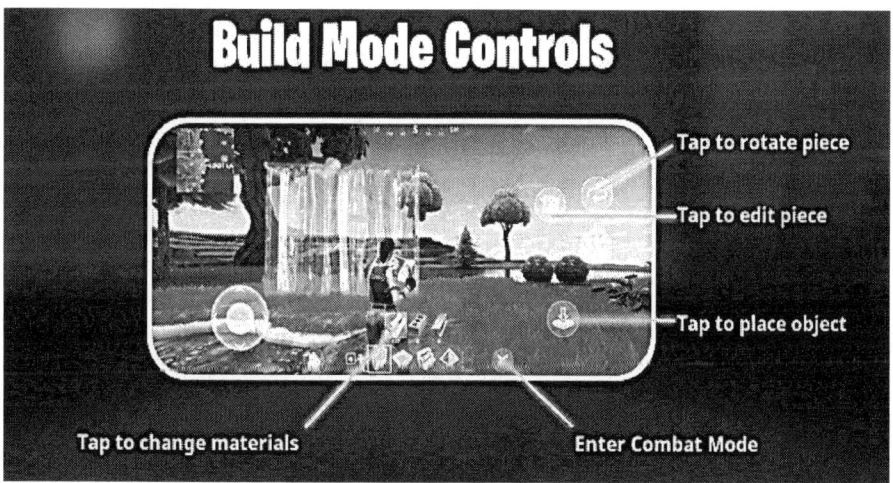

Basics

Game Modes

1.   Solo:

A solo match is the most challenging one. All 100 players are thirsty for each other's blood. The layer who survives every other player wins the match. In solo, you are an ally of yourself only. Your main goal is to stay alive until the end of the match.

It is considered cheating if you unofficially team up with other players for survival. Playing solo is very stressful. It is you against the world and there is no one to guide you through the game. To help you against a situation like this, we have hidden scenarios and strategies in our content, read it through and you would need no help.

2.   Duo:

In duo mode, you are allowed to pair up and battle against 49 other players. Although, there are still more enemies than in squad, however, there is a teammate that you can always rely on.

As compare to solo it is a lot less stressful and fun to play. You can make great strategies through mutual discussion. Communication is the key when it comes to choosing a target location and aiming at buildings and spots. If you suddenly spot an enemy or you are in trouble, you always have someone to call to.

Make sure you both are looting as much material as you can. Be it from chopping the trees or gathering from fallen enemies. Resources always come in handy. The best strategy in the duo is keeping a distance when fighting, looting or traveling. It is to ensure that you both don't die at the same time and this opens bigger ambushing opportunities.

3.   Squad:

Fortnite: Battle Royale is a different experience when playing in a squad. The group play allows up to 5 players to team up. They can be friends from before, squad formed by making match or players placed together to form a team. The initial ratio of players is still 100, by making groups of 5 there are 20 teams to battle against. The game is more relaxed but also more strategized because now there are 5 brains working to achieve a common goal.

4.   Limited time modes :

Epic Games recently confirmed that Limited time game modes will be occasionally made available. At present, the team of 20 (placing 20 players in 5 large teams) is available for limited time. Previously LTM's have lasted for approximately a week.

This is a muddled mode with large battles. You can practice your skills on these modes without being vulnerable.

Following are the upcoming LTMs. The date of their release has not yet been announced.

Blitz Mode:

•   This offers fast and shorter matches;

•   Drop into the first circle – Start your game from a specific area instead of jumping into the whole circle;

•   Storm radius decreasing faster than its usual speed;

50v50 v2:

- Two teams with 50 players each battle for survival. Each team has its own resources and the combats are deadlier.

Another mode is known as a **Solid Gold** mode. This mode is only available for teams. Its main theme revolves are collecting legendary weapons. For the length of mode, every weapon found in chests or around the map will be of legendary variety such as Rocket Launcher, Minigun, Sniper Rifle and the lately introduced Hand Cannon.

The Storm Eye

Since the objective of the game is last man, team or duo standing, many may choose to hide until the rest have been killed. To avoid a situation like this Storm eye plays a huge role. It keeps players on their toes.

- In order to stay safe, you have to stay inside the storm eye;
- At the start the storm eye covers the whole map;
- The storm keeps on tapering throughout the game;
- Shrinking of storm happens in two phases which has its own timer. First, the map shows the area where the storm shrinks second the storm actually starts shrinking;
- If you are out in the storm you will keep on taking damage until you die;
- Storm eye is vital for survival.

Tips for managing The Storm Eye:

Since staying in the storm eye is of ultimate importance, many players stay around the edge of the circle and keep on moving with perimeter as it shrinks. However, this strategy may work for a while but can't last as the game progresses. At that point you do need to build a solid base, using your most durable resources.

Using weaker building material will make it easy for your opponent to break through. To manage the storm eye, you must be aware of your position relative to the circle. Be quick to move on as you don't want to get caught up in the battle while the storm eye is shrinking. It will take a bit of practice to make it work though.

Starting Location

Starting location sets the tone for the rest of your game. For instance, if you have landed in a populated area of the city, you have more weapons and objects to loot. The risk, however, is that you might end up against an enemy who possesses much deadlier weapon than yours.

Contrary to that, you might consider starting from a quieter portion of the map. Surely, you would have to travel to loot, but it will lend you enough time to set up strategies and you can know the terrain.

There are loot chests around the map. Regardless of the area you land, keep your ear open for any tingling noise. If you hear one, search for it, as its highly probable you will find valuable material in it. The rarity of the item in the chest is not dependent on the location. You might find a top-tier weapon in the places you least expect.

There are 20 separate regions for exploring on Fortnite:

Each region offers unique opportunities for looting and close combat. Some regions are popular, so when you land on any of those, remember to stay ready for battle right away.

We have broken down some areas of the map and information on each terrain to make things easy for you.

Anarchy Acres:

It is a good place to take the start from. It is a rural location, full of farmyards, fields as well as buildings which contain a chest or two. It is rumored that backside of northern-most houses has extra ammo and a chest, you can definitely confirm that. Search through the barns, haystacks, houses. Also, break-down other materials as they often hold chests.

Dusty Depot:

This is an industrial area located in the heart of the map. It has warehouses full of stolen goods, chests, and building materials. Don't forget to explore the warehouses. They often have high-tier loot located in these spots.

Fatal Fields:

It is a farm area near anarchy acres in Fortnite: Battle Royale positioned at the southern section of the map. Check all the buildings and especially under the bridge for loot and chests. Since there are a lot of vehicles nearby this is also a good place to gather metals.

Flush Factory:

It is in the south-west corner of the map. It is a heavy industrial and densely built-up area. While it is full of chests and equipment to loot be careful about the popular areas, as you are likely to encounter enemies there. This is a place you should consider going after landing nearby when the rush has subsided.

Greasy Grove:

It is a residential area, located towards the south-west area of the map. It has a restaurant, a gas station along with houses. It is an active spot for early game activity so, beware.

Haunted Hills:

This place is in the south. Rummage around inside the Mausoleum to get valuable objects. However, keep an eye on the circle as you are right on the edge of the map.

Lonely Lodge:

This area has numerous huts hiding a lot of chests. This is a good starting point for players who want to play safe. You can find a good amount of metal from here. Check out the towers, it often has a chest or two.

Loot Lake:

It is a watery place except on big old mansion in the middle. It contains plenty of loot and up to four chests. Check the roofs, insides of building and boats as well. It is popular landing spot and can attract heavy combat.

Lucky Landing:

It is in the southern part of the map. It is an Asian-themed are which is represented by a huge cherry tree in the middle. It is a small area on the map which consists of some small buildings which circle around a larger town hall. Although it looks gorgeous, you will hardly find any loot there.

Moisty Mire:

This damp and dirty swamp area is positioned near Fatal Fields in the south-east segment of the map. It is a good location to gather lots of wood, you can also find a chest or two, but that is not probable. It is also a less popular zone and starting from here can be a good choice.

Pleasant Park:

It is in the north-west section of the map. Tremendous looting opportunities from houses around it.

Retail Row:

This complex area is located towards the map and is very popular for getting started. There are several opportunities for looting. Don't forget to dig the vehicles sprayed around it.

Resources

Resources in Battle Royale can either be found lying on the ground or hidden in a chest. Another way is to mine the resources by hitting trees and rocks with a pickaxe.

Unfortunately for you, picking these items can create some noise which might warn a nearby enemy of your location. In order to avoid this scenario, search the area and play close attention to sounds of battle nearby. If you are 100% sure that you are alone in the area, only then start looting.

You may think of skipping these stuff for fear of exposing yourself, however, you do need to build defensive structures on the advanced stages of the game when the battles are even more lethal. It is wiser to get resources on any opportunity that you can get. If you ever want to be among the top players, you need to be good at building structures.

The most common resource is wood, and a certain limit is given to every player by default. Because of its abundance, you will come across plenty of wooden building, outpost, and myriad trees. On the other hand, massive buildings like shelters can also be advantageous which are built through high-end resources like brick and metal.

Gathering weapons early can result in greater stability in the game. Since that is the time most players don't have access to deadly weapons and you can easily gain an upper edge.

Traps

We will go to the gun part later, first look the possible traps we can choose from. There is a fair number of items that you can gather as you move around the map. These items can provide major advantages on the battlefield. They can even get you a perfect camouflage.

Traps can be used as a ploy against your enemy by luring them into killing themselves. These items can be placed on a plane surface to get aide in the battle.

Below is the list of traps in Fortnite Battle Royale.

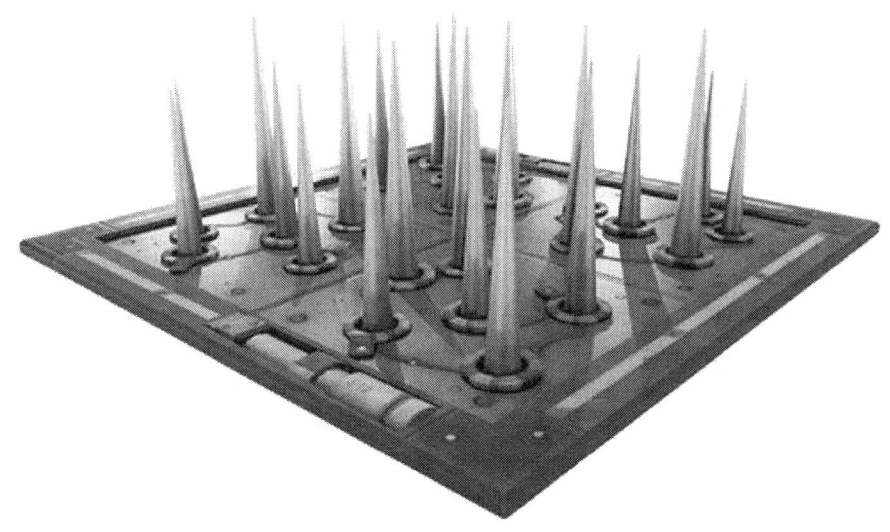

Damage Trap:

Damage Trap is designed by combining the functions of Spike Trap, Wall Zapper and Ceiling Zapper from the Fortnite game. Whether you place it on the floor or any other building parts, it will automatically change places from one location to another. In simple words, it keeps on changing its location.

Launch Pad:

It is a magic device that will either help you escape or will take you away from the shrinking storm. Level up the floor and place your launch pad on it. Jump on it and it will boost you to the air, place your glider and land wherever you want.

Cozy Campfire:

This one is a rare healing floor trap. You can find it anywhere. Cozy Campfire persists for 25 seconds and healing 2 HP per second.

Best Weapons

There is an absolutely long list of weapons in Fortnite: Battle Royale. However, not all of them are as good as the one we have chosen. To gain an upper hand and to win, you must have solid weapon base.

You'll come across and even possess close-range shotguns and long-range assault and sniper rifles, pistols, SMGs, and rarely rocket launchers and more. Weapons also have scarcity classifications: Weapons with white ribbon around them are the most common and weakest ones in the game, the green ones are a little better than white ones, blue is good enough, purple is better, orange is best, and gold is the ultimate weapon. As a rule, the higher the tier the better the gun. The downside is, at the start, it is impossible to know whether the rifle that you see is worth a pick or not. Given below are the list of weapons and reasons why we call them the best.

Note: This list is just one of our favorites. We absolutely don't want to make a hard and fast rule to acquire these. You can choose one based on your comfort and strategy. It is simply a list of weapons we have the most success with.

M16/Assault Rifle:

For short range to mid-range battle, M16 is a decent choice. If shots are placed accurately it is effective to take down the enemy. However, when it comes to long-range battles it might swivel a bit. The more you hold the trigger the wider its bullet spread goes.

The solution is to tap the trigger lightly, but you must be accurate with your target if you want to impose harm.

Pump/Tactical Shotgun:

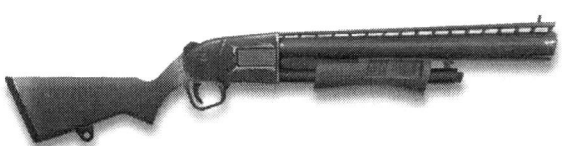

These are perfect tools for close range combat. The pump has a slower fire rate, but a perfect hit is good enough to blow the enemy in one-shot (again, to take full advantage you need a good aim). In the present game, you can lessen the time to reload by keeping two in stock. When one runs out you can surprise with another one. It may take some time to get used to of this technique. On the other hand, the Tactical shotgun has much higher fire rate and is more damaging. It is easier to use, and you don't need to have a master aim in order to relish its potential.

Bolt Action/Semi-Auto Sniper Rifle:

Having a sniper in the backpack can increase your chances of victory. Landing a headshot with a sniper will eliminate your enemy in an instant, provided you have a good aim. As the circle shrinks, combat increases, holding a sniper while you are in a safe position lets you spot and eliminate target as they come.

Bolt version stands out as compared to semi-auto. With Bolt, every shot counts. However, with semi-auto, you are likely to stand still and spamming shots. This highlights our position that is disadvantageous to us.

Rocket Launcher:

It is a destruction tool. It might not be a perfect fit for close combat but when it comes to destroying forts it has no alternative. It is great for attacking a group of enemies or taking their covers off. Rocket Launcher has limited ammo so gather as much as you can.

SCAR/Assault Rifle:

It is one of the most lethal weapons of the game. It is a gun that will handle any situation you throw at it. It has outstanding accuracy, higher DPS and can be used for all ranges. SCAR only comes as an EPIC or Legendary, the best way to grab it, is looting out chests or fallen enemies.

Health Recovery

Bandage:

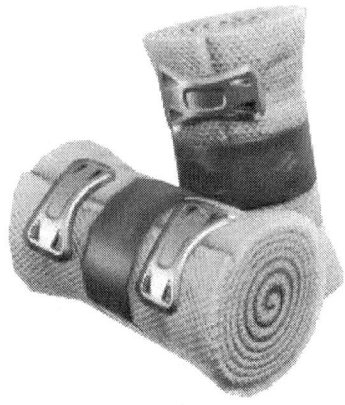

The oldest healing method in the game. It is capable of healing only 15 points each time when used. This makes it less desirable when compared with other healing items (mentioned below). The only times 15 points make a difference is when your enemy has less than you.

Bandages are present almost everywhere in the map. Bear in mind though that they rack up as much inventory space as other healing items. When you find a better option don't think twice to replace it with the bandages.

Small Shield Potions:

This potion provides you with an extra shield. However, mini version takes 2 seconds to drink and recovers on 25 points of the shield. They can be found in a pack of three.

Large Shield Potions:

It increases your personal shield up to 50 points. Drinking a pair of them will take it up to 100. It takes five seconds to drink and they can be found quite often to be considered as rare items. However, mini shield potions are more in abundance as compared to large shield potions.

Slurp Juice:

It is a heal-over-time potion. It gives you a total of 1-point health and 1-point shield for a total of 25 seconds. It can fully restore your health if you have the capacity to get there.

Chug-jug:

It gets the player maximum health and shielding that he needs. However, it takes 15-seconds to drink and you might be vulnerable to an attack. Look for a safe and quiet location to drink it in.

How to Build

To make things easy we would recommend you re-bind your keys. By default, the crafting mechanics are all linked to function keys which takes a bit time to grab on to. You can save time by setting up building options 2 and 3 near to WASD keys. This way you will craft quicker and get better results.

Basics:

- The Q key is set to building walls. You will see a blue template where the wall or another structure will be placed.

- Click on the location where you want to place structure.

- Ramps, platforms etc. can also be linked to your other buildings. You will see a blueprint every time when you are placing new attachments.

- The template will turn red when a place is not suitable for a structure.

- You need an adequate amount of resources (read above) in order to build. Thee right screen will show the icons necessary for building.

- To swap the building material, click the right mouse button.

- To edit or delete an existing structure press G.

How to craft:

To craft you need materials, once you have gathered those, go to your inventory and choose the item (traps or defenses) you want to craft. Once the item is selected, you will see a list of materials that you need and those you already have. After that, just click on craft button or press C. Give it few seconds and you will see the item in your inventory.

To see the weapon and trap material collection, go to the collection book beneath the armory section of the menu.

Structure crafting is different from weapon crafting. To switch from weapons, structure or trap placement press Q. Structure building requires space such as a connection on the ground or any other structure. Again, you need materials for building. you can customize structures but pressing G.

Daily and Weekly Challenges

Fortnite: Battle Royale comes with weekly or daily challenges to complete. These challenges comprise of tasks such as taking out competition using a specific weapon a certain number of times or outlive a certain number of players etc.

Some of these tasks may take some time to complete which lets you stock up to three tasks at a time. You can receive one extra daily challenge if you have an active Battle Pass, you can also have four tasks stacked at the same time. We have tried to list down several daily challenges you will encounter throughout the game. Again, don't forget they may be subject to change since the game is regularly updated.

Outlive Solo Players:

Objective: Survive player in a solo queue.

This task is done solo as the name suggest. You have to outlive150 other players. The best trick of survival is to avoid conflict. The longer you last the faster you will accomplish your objective.

Outlive Squad Players:

Objective: to live longer than other players in the Duo mode.

This is similar to the above with a little difference. Yes, that's right, you must survive longer than 150 players while in a squad mode.

Outlive Players:

Objective: Outlive 200 players.

Just as the one before, this time only it is 200 players. The longer you stay the more progress you will make. Again, the tip is same for this that is avoid trouble.

Sniper Rifle Eliminations:

Objective: Kills others using your Sniper Rifle.

Use this challenge to perfect your aim. The task is simple, you have to kill 5 other players using only your Sniper Rifle. The more you get used to of the weapon, the easier it will be to play and win. Solo modes are best for speedy kills, knockdowns won't help to complete challenges.

Assault Rifle Eliminations:

Objective: Use assault Rifle to kill other players.

Just like the above challenge, you have to pick up 5 players and kill them with an Assault Rifle. This time you need to be the aggressor as oppose to hiding out.

SMG Eliminations:

Objective: Use SMG to kill other players.

Just like the above, this one is the same, you need to wipe five other players with SMG to accomplish this task. This one can be a little scary as you have to get closer to your enemy for a quick kill. The tip is to find SMG early in the game when other enemies are still looking for armor, kill and win.

Search Chests:

Objective: Find five chests.

This task is easy, all you must do is hunt five chests and done! Try starting from the less populated areas of the map, get comfortable with the area. You will have a bigger chance of finding chests in that area without getting killed. One of the locations for this is Snobby Shore, it is not very populated and has surprisingly plenty of chests. Forget about killing and avoid getting killed. Just hunt down the chests and job well done.

Search Ammo Boxes:

Objective: Hunt Ammo Boxes.

They are tiny dark boxes hidden throughout the map. The task is to search and open a certain number of them. You can search different houses as they often carry those items. Avoid battles as much as possible.

Play 3 Matches:

Objective: Play 3-matches.

As you can guess, this challenge is simple. You just have to play a total of three games in any modes. It stacks pretty well with the other tasks. Keep in mind that quitting the task wouldn't always count. You can also complete the task by either killing yourself or jump into heavy battlefield areas.

Place Top 6 in Squads:

Objective: Be part of remaining top 6 squads.

You already know what it means. Remember, in order to accomplish this task, you have to play in the squad. You just have to survive long enough that only 5 more teams are remaining.

All the above tasks are easy to accomplish and will give you a lot of practice for the actual game.

A new Daily Contest will come up each day at the same time for the switchover is 4:00 pm PST. That's 7:00 pm EST, 12:00 am in the UK and 1:00 am in Europe.

If you are really not interested in completing the task. Then, go to the menu, select "inspect Challenges" and then leave the one you don't want to keep anymore. You will not be getting any new ones until the next reset, so don't let go of XP-earning opportunities.

Completing daily challenges will get you 500 experience points. Not only that you will become more aware of the map and it is also a great opportunity to practice your aim and other gaming skills.

Note: *Your season level increases through experience points. Progress in your season level gets you more Battle Stars. You battle pass will get upgraded through this.*

Here is a comprehensive list of weekly challenges we have come across. Again, since the game keeps on updating there are more likely to come.

Week 2 Challenges

- Practice a Launchpad (5 Battle Stars)
- Inflict damage with Assault Rifles to foes (5 Battle Stars)
- Search in Sobbing Woods (5 Battle Stars)
- Dance in different prohibited locations (5 Battle Stars)
- Explore between a Pool, Windmill and an Umbrella (10 Battle Stars)
- SMG kills (10 Battle Stars)
- Eliminate enemies in Greasy Grove (10 Battle Stars)

Week 3 Challenges

- Stock building resources with a pickaxe (5 Battle Stars)
- Inflict damage through Repressed Weapons to opponents (5 Battle Stars)
- Hunt Chests in Junk Junction (5 Battle Stars)
- Land on various Bullseyes (5 Battle Stars)

- Survey the treasure map which is found in Snobby Shores (10 Battle Stars)
- Crossbow Exclusions (10 Battle Stars)
- Eliminate Enemies in Salty Springs (10 Battle Stars)

Week 4 Challenges

- Inflict damage with Sniper Rifles to challengers (5 Battle Stars)
- Hunt Supply Drops (5 Battle Stars)
- Find Chests in Flush Factory (5 Battle Stars)
- Visit various Ice Cream Trucks (5 Battle Stars)
- Hunt between a Vehicle Tower, Rock Sculpture, and a Circle of Hedges (10 Battle Stars)
- Trap Removals (10 Battle Stars)
- Eliminate Enemies in Tomato Town (10 Battle Stars)

Week 5 Challenges

- Practice the Bush (0/1). 5 Battle Points
- Hunt treasure chests in Moisty Mire (0/7). 5 Battle Points
- Damage your enemies using pickaxe (0/200). 5 Battle Points
- Visit various Gas Stations in a single match (0/3). 5 Battle Points
- Follow the treasure map hidden in the anarchy acres - HARD (0/1). 10 Battle Points
- Exclude pistols - HARD (0/3). 10 Battle Points
- Eliminate enemies present in the Tilted Towers - HARD (0/3). 10 Battle Points.

Before the First Match

Before you begin the match, we have highlighted some key tricks to adopt that will save you a lot of trouble in the future play. Even if you have played it before, this is something you should read.

- As the match begins and you are thrown out of the plane, it is important to get your hands on as much loot as you can. In order to succeed you need a lot of weapon and building resources for both, the initial and the lateral stage of the game;

- For weapons try to get your hands-on Shotgun, an Assault Rifle, and a Sniper Rifle. These three weapons are an excellent starter choice for your future battles. These tools will surely execute damage on any encounter;

- There are variations in the Sniper Rifle, ideally, you should aim for Bolt-Action version of the weapon. Although these weapons can take some time to adjust to, however, once you clear your aim, you will be laughing as you move to the next battle.

Here is the list of items listed in priority order to get your hands on!

- Shotgun;
- Assault Rifle;
- Sniper;
- Meds;
- Shield.

In order to win the game other items are also necessary, you can always loot them on luxury. However, these pieces are important in strategizing your win. You should learn to wield them well, otherwise, you can never use their true potential. Rocket launchers can also come in handy and are useful for taking out late-game bases but in the earlier stages of the game, they should rest well beneath the list.

Movement and Environment:

If you are a PUBG player, you need to re-wire your game to the new meta when it comes to mapping traversal. Like mentioned earlier, objects can be transformed into resources, you have the option to build stairs and get up sloped areas efficiently. The sooner you get used to of it the better strategies you can make.

Always think about your weakness and how you can cover it. Keep building battle strategies in your mind. For instance, if you come under heavy fire, you can gain upper hand by building walls around yourself.

On the defensive side, remember to avoid any irrational move, especially when you are charging into a building. If the building is already occupied the person inside is going to be aware of your location, while you, on the other hand, are totally clueless about theirs. If you know someone inside, be patient and wait for them to come out, launch a surprise attack and job done! Seeking them out is always the bad news.

If you don't have any other option but to go in, use the building materials that you have gathered and create a structure that wraps around the building. Through this, you can take them from above and gain advantage without any compromise on your security.

Map Strategy:

There are two strategies that can be very helpful to assure success in Fortnite: Battle Royale.

- Big Kill strategy:

This strategy takes a lot of skill and luck, but it is definitely worth it. In this, your approach is very aggressive, you stay at the edge and wait for players as they rush towards the center of the circle escaping from the storm. However, it has a very high risk of you getting caught up in the storm yourself.

- Safe play:

This is a passive approach as compared to the first one. This is all about running to the center of new circle immediately and from there on charge and kill. Once you have positioned yourself, you can take advantage of the area and plan your attacks accordingly.

Avoid entering the circle from a wrong angle, where you can easily be spotted and killed. Instead, rush to the center by doing so you can get to view the whole terrain, its good and bad spots and set up a base before your enemy comes.

The best place to position yourself is the high grounds. The location itself gives you an advantage over your enemy and also gives you an opportunity to run away if the battle does not go your way.

This is both a defense and something to expect when enemy attacks. Making way up the slope can be easily done through crafts and this can put you in a favorable position as well as worst position. It is wise to always have a defense strategy.

When traversing the map be keen towards your surroundings. If you look around there are many visual and audio cues that will aid you to get intel about someone. If you feel that you are not alone in the area, then crouch because it will hush your footsteps. Then you can cleverly pinpoint your enemy through the sound it produces and prepares a surprise but lethal attack.

Resources:

Always use your resources wisely. You should have enough to at least build an emergency wall. Avoid battles if you are short of resources. You should always have up to 300 pieces of resources stacked in your in your inventory.

Chasing, killing and bagging the deadliest weapons is necessary but while doing so don't underestimate the power of resources. Your defensive strategies should be as good as your offensive strategies.

Try your level best to avoid situations where you would have to build structures in an emergency. Whether its hyper setting ramps for an opponent or constructing walls to shelter from the attack, if you are out of resources, then run as fast as you can!

Wood is a great resource for quick building objects, however, stone and metal are brilliant for building a strong fort in later stages.

Tips, Tricks, and Secrets

We have summarized some general tips and tricks to ensure your position in the top players of the game.

• If you hear another battle around you- contemplate into going there. See if you can defeat them, however also keep in mind that your enemy might have much stronger weapons than yours. Or if you can't resist, try attacking at the end of the battle when almost both the participants are hurt. The reward of bringing down other players can be something to look forward to such as rare weapons, more shields etc. The situation can always reverse too.

• It is highly recommended to use headphones while playing. It lets you hear even the slightest of sound and you can always counter a surprise attack. In Fortnite the sound of movement is much louder, which gives you enough time to zero in on your enemies.

• Weapon and resources appear more frequently in popular areas. However, we totally don't suggest you start from there at all. Since, a lot of players aim to those areas, getting into an early combat is highly probable. See the risk and reward of situations like these. It's better to get familiar with your environment, build up resources traverse the map and once you are settled get ready for a combat.

• Players often close the door after entering a room or building. This is a deceptive way which makes another player think no one has entered the room or building, while you are all set for a surprise attack. Or you can keep the door open to trick another player into thinking that the house has already been looted. You can also fall for the same trick so be cautious when you see either.

- Ideally, you should gather long-range weapons. Rifles are good for mid-range while sniper is great for long range. Finding healing items is rare, however, having a bandage or med-kit can come in handy.

Tips for Beginners

Build Your Chances of Survival

As you already know that the last man, team or duo standing is the winner. Although it's similar to PUBG, there are plenty of small differences that make it stand out from the base game. Knowing when and what move to make will get you last in the game.

There is no tutorial to start with so when you land on one of its islands, you have to quickly start looting whatever comes your way. Throughout our guide we have been leaving tips and tricks but here is a more compiled version of possible tips we have gathered to get you starting and possibly winning.

We have tips for beginners, advanced and experts. So, skip to any of these levels and get a dose full of tips.

Pick Your Landing Zone and Avoid Other Players

Knowing where you land creates a big impact on the rest of your game. As you are competing against 99 other players, carefully check out the map and avoid getting into an early combat.

Your first priority should be to gather as many weapons as you can. Above, we have gathered a list of weapons that are must have in your game. Try to look for those weapons and avoid combat with other players.

Weapons can be mostly found in building, try to avoid popular spots as it has a bigger chance of combat. Pick a less popular location. These places also have great gear and you can get comfortable before you break into a fight. You can also delay your jumps for a few seconds and spot where you want to land. Stay away from the wild crowd which usually jumps just as the door opens. You can set waypoints on your map screen which makes it easier to trace any structures or settlements you have chosen for looting.

You will skydive through the plane, you can locate the area you want to land on and then deploy your glider towards that direction. Don't take too long though, the faster you reach the ground the more looting you can do. Make sure you keep your eyes and ears open for any signs of the enemy around you. Remember, your goal is to survive, as a beginner, you should focus on looting and getting at the center of the storm eye. Avoid combat as much as you can, by the time the game gets messier you will have enough resources to get into combat and emerge victoriously. Of course, it's easier said than done, you would need a lot of practice to succeed.

The Storm Is Your Greatest Enemy

As mentioned before, The Storm is the mechanic of the Fortnite. A timer is present at the corner of the screen which will indicate the time left for storm contraction. The timer at the corner of your screen will note the storm contraction. As the game progresses the storm will grow smaller and the players will get closer to each other making battles more lethal.

No matter what you are busy with never forget the timer. You can't just run at the center and stay there because as the circle contacts its center changes. The movement of the circle means that you have to run to save yourself from the storm. Always know where you need to be, the best practice is to always get to your destination quickly.

Gather Resources First

When you first land the only armor, you will have is a pickaxe. Although initially, you can fight people with it, later it is not the that effective, especially when you enemy possess a gun. The main use of pickaxe is to break into structures and gather resources. Every time you break and gather resources, you are bound to create noise. While you are destroying vehicles, you have an extra risk of triggering an alarm, which will warn others.

For starters, break walls, structures and trees, gather at least 300 units of wood. This will get you key materials for survival. If you shift to the building menu you will realize that few structures can be recycled such as floors, roof, walls, and stairs. It is safer to gather materials early in the game rather than later when the battles are inevitable and more intense.

Practice Building (Especially Under Fire)

With resources, you can start a few matches learning ways in which buildings can help. Building structures are the best form of defense and creative structures will help you change the map and provide cover in a firefight. This does not mean to build in every situation, you need to your resources for the right moment and built whenever you really need. Just be comfortable with the tools.

Building structures start automatically once you choose a weapon. This means that even when you are under heavy fire you can easily build to take cover. You can build a wall which will take the bullets while you go to a favorable spot. Through Ramps, you can pass impossible terrain and gives you quick high ground to take advantage of. Although, you shouldn't solely rely on it as it is used in combination with other tactics but it's one to root for.

Remember one thing, building a structure creates noise which can leave you vulnerable. You can easily spot fortification build by other players. Every resource supply has its pros and cons, the stronger a metal the more time it takes to construct them which often leaves you out in the open. These sturdier metals are also hard to find, while wood is more common. When you are under fire and you need a cover, wood is the best option. You should save brick and metal for the end-game when fights are expected to be more lethal.

Gear Up

As soon as you land start searching for weapons. Weapons go into any of five inventory spots located at the bottom of the screen. You'll want to get equipped with whatever you can find right away, however, don't hesitate to drop things when you find better weapons. Rare weapons are usually more accurate and more potent and come with additions like silencers or scopes. If you find a rare gun just swap it with the common gun without giving it a second thought.

Keep Quiet

As the play area shrinks, the players will get closer to each other. This means they will be able to hear you moving around, shooting or building. Sound is vital to secure victory, good speakers and headphones are recommended to help you detect even lightest of sound.

Don't Fight Unless you are Sure of Victory

Firefights in Fortnite can be a bit deceptive. They start out looking like victories and suddenly change their course and become nightmares. A surprise attack will always leave your enemy baffled but the situation can always take a turn for the worst. Your biggest plus always surprises, but you only have one life. It is important to know when to attack and when to just ignore. If you are not entirely confident about taking down a player, it's important to just let them be and move on, instead of attacking and risking it all.

It is important to have a good aim at Fortnite, failure in aim can alert your enemy and the favorable situation can turn against you. It is important to know the distance from you can the target and have the right gun for the distance. However, a normal gun will do just fine in close combat battles. While for the long-range Battles Assault Rifle or Sniper Rifles are the best option and get your players before they can respond.

Take down your enemy by surprise, you can do this by staying calm, align your shot and make sure your enemy is not too far away. Survival is your most vital goal, so be discrete: If you're not assured that you will be able to take down whoever's in your view quickly and neatly, you're perhaps better off by letting them go.

Be Careful in The Open

The mechanics are not hidden, you often must run in the open to make it inside the circle. However, it opens you to more dangerous, because it makes you visible no matter how much you bend. So, when moving in the open choosing the right path is of utmost importance. Top tier players always avoid running in the open and quickly change their direction from one spot to another.

Use cliffs, rocks and buildings as cover, shield yourself and keep close on watch on your surroundings. When you are in the open grounds move as fast as you can, however, reverse your strategy when you are hiding, move as slowly as possible. You're harmless when you're not in action. Hiding in pine trees and scrubs are good camouflaging spots. Through third-person perspective, you can place your character in such a way that you can look through entrances and corners before you proceed to enter. This will help you avoid walking into traps or players hiding away from sight.

Watch for Player Buildings

As the game progresses, you're likely to see player fortifications. Player buildings are typically square, blank, obvious towers, so you will usually spot them from a distance. These are clear indicators that players are stacked there. So, if you come across any defense structure, approach it with caution (avoid it if you have an option). They're clear signs of where players are camping, so if you ever see a tower or other defenses, you should totally approach them with caution. It is a clear sign that someone is waiting with an Assault Rifle and will hunt anyone who crosses.

Steer clear of it if you spot one. Usually, huge constructions show that player is well stocked, in other words, they are well equipped for an attack, especially since if they are at a high position they already have a bigger battle benefit than you. If you're intending to fight someone in a tower or other building, you're going to need strong or stronger weapon. The recent update on miniguns and rare rocket launchers can blow constructions like a fly. You should always stock the right tools for the job.

Never Trust Cover

Every defense is destructible. Whether they are players or constructions, everything is fallible. Even the existing constructions on the map are destructible. So, do not totally rely on taking cover. Constructions are good for giving temporary cover but not for long-term purpose. Use these constructions to take a moment and make a new plan.

Be Careful When Looting Defeated Players

It is always fun to bring down another player as it means you are one step closer to victory. On those moments, where you might feel a little arrogant as well, don't let your guards down because you have not yet won the match. Keep in mind that every time you shoot from your gun, you expose your location as the gun sound can be heard far enough. You are likely to attract an enemy or alert those who are hiding nearby. Getting cocky at that moment can be head-blowing which means the end of the game for you.

Tips for Advanced Players

Not only do you need to outwit and outgun other players, you also need to efficiently use your building abilities to traverse the map, fortify your spots, and beat out the rivals.

Players who've been around the block in Fortnite's single-player crusade have no doubt selected a lot of strategies, and pieces of information that can help uplift them to multiplayer victory. For everybody else, it can be hard to pick up on all Fortnite's peculiarities and concealed bits of information especially since the free Battle Royale mode doesn't play a tutorial. Use these tips to get an advantage over the other 99 opponents in your Fortnite: Battle Royale match.

Use Headphones

It really is hard to overestimate how vital sound is in Fortnite. You will use it to catch individuals sneaking up on you, surprise on enemies who are firing at you, and trail players for ambushes. It is a hindrance to listening to the game over your computer and TV speakers, or even a complete sound system, in contrast to players who are equipped with a quality pair of sound headphones. The sound is perhaps the best tool in your game in Fortnite, so make sure you're able to use it as efficiently as possible.

Speed Is Key Early On

As you get comfortable with the map, you will want to stride as fast as you can to find quality arms early. That begins with your jump from the game's soaring party bus at the start of each match: If you're poised in your aggressive abilities, pick a spot with lots of structures, and glide straight for it. Avoid dropping over hills and other high-elevation zones, as these will make your glider to auto-deploy rather than if you dive toward lower-elevation areas like water or canyons. The inspiration is to fall to earth as swiftly as you can so that you can outsmart other players with the guns and bring them down.

While it's best for new players to shut doors behind them to guard themselves, once you're used to the tide of the game, you don't have to stress about hiding yourself almost as much. Get into some constructions, find what's valuable, and move on as quickly as you can as the old' "loot and scoot" approach. Getting high-quality weapons early will set you up for achievement against players who have feebler gear than you, so get used to running on to new locations rapidly and looting as much and as quickly as you can. Just be careful about it, so that you don't run into an ambush.

Don't Pick Up Everything

One of the best habits you can adopt as you progress your Fortnite career is to be discriminating about what to choose up and what to ignore behind. It's appealing to take up everything you come across as you never know when you may need to want to shift between a pistol, a rifle, and a shotgun, right?

Though, you will possibly use one or two guns for most of your match, except when you've got the rarer and more powerful ones like sniper rifles, miniguns, and rocket launchers. Taking a handful of white or green pistols that you don't mean to use will just slug you down when it comes time to shift out for better loot. As an alternative, make quick choices about what is essential and what is not, and act consequently.

Stopping to organize your inventory can leave you exposed, so take only what you really need, and learn to disregard the less useful loot.

Note: While you must hand-pick up weapons and objects, ammo gets chosen up automatically. So, if you're looking at a mass of loot and all you want are the ammunition, save time by just striding over it to avoid unintentionally picking up the wrong stuff.

Double Up Your Guns for Added Damage

While you're being discriminating about what guns you pick up, know that two of the same weapon can be useful, mostly when it comes to the thrust shotgun and the bolt-action sniper rifle. By taking two of these guns next to in inventory spaces, you can overcome the wait between shotgun pumps or sniper reloads, and in its place just shift to your second type of the gun to fire a second shot instantly. The quick shift can be hard to get used to, but with the supremacy that this move gives you, it's worth training yourself to shift rather than wait for a reload. It's an awesome way to maximize your fierceness against other players.

Chop Down Trees for More Wood

Where you get your resources matters. Particularly early on, you want to take as much wood as you can, as it's highly valuable in battles and for defense. You can smash down buildings and break down boxes of wood with your pickaxe but as it ensures, these have less wood than trees. By choosing the right tree, and you can collect up to 40-plus units of wood from a solo node, swiftly filling up your materials and giving you abundant from just a tweak. Pine trees whose green portions range close to the ground incline to be the best, but it's worth testing as you play, to learn where on the atlas you can get the most materials quickest.

The same can be said for other materials. Brick walls give some brick, but heaps of rocks out in the wilds are even better. You can also get a good haul of metal from demolishing vehicles, but be suspicious: Sometimes, breaking up a car will set off its alarm, which can lure other players to your location.

Wood Trumps Metal (In Certain Cases)

Usually, wood is considered as the weakest material, while brick as a stronger, and metal as the strongest. In reality, this means that wood buildings can take the smallest amount of damage before they break down overall, brick constructions have more strength than wood, and metal buildings have the most durability. Heavier materials come with disadvantages, though. Brick structures take a longer time to build and reach full potential than wood buildings do, and metal takes the longest in comparison.

Take (Or Build) The High Ground

Elevated ground will win you battles in Fortnite, and that doesn't just count high hills or cliffs, though these offer better vantage points in overall. In firefights, practice upward building as quickly as you can. You can make walls and then ramps to guard yourself as you climb and firing down on other players gets you more headshots and destruction while giving you better defense. Quickly build a ramp fenced by walls means lets you jump up and take headshots at opponents below while also making yourself tough to hit.

When you can, shape up for the benefit and if the other player is making efforts to get above you, try to get even higher or force them to alter locations, to take their lead away. Don't forget to quickly build wood walls in front of your ramps, in case the other player flash them out from under you. Striking the bottom of a ramp will ruin it, and the injury you take from falling could cost you the fight and match as well.

Watch For (And Mark) Supply Drops

Every so often, the soaring bus will drop a source crate. The crates' drop places are marked by blue smoke bombs on the ground, and they hover down on balloons once they're released. These crates hold some of the best loot in the game, as well as the minigun and rocket launcher, so they're absolutely worth your attention but they're expected to attract other players, too.

Complete Daily Challenges to Earn V-Bucks

V-Bucks are Fortnite's exclusive currency, which can be used to buy cosmetic objects to make your player wear cooler clothes or install more fun emotes. Buying with real money will get you a hefty number of V-bucks to use. If you're ready to put in the time, it's also probable to earn some just by playing the game, however, it will take you a while.

Playing Fortnite gets you experience points on the basis of your performance in a match, and each time you get enough, you level up, which gets you one "Battle Star." After taking 10 Battle Stars, you progress to a new "tier," and after a certain tier, you get new emotes and other items. It's likely to earn tiers faster by finishing Daily Challenges (explained above), which are enumerated on the home screen when you log into Fortnite. Contests require you to complete different actions, like killing a set quantity of players with a specific gun. Tasks give you a cluster of experience points and five Battle Stars for finishing them, which can benefit you to earn tiers a lot faster.

Tips for Experts

Be Very Wary of Open Doors

Open doors are famous for trouble. When you come across one chance are it's already cleaned (no need to spend time) or someone is inside to welcome you with loads of bullet. Sometimes it can also mean that someone is there busy looting, which gives you an opportunity for a surprise attack.

What if danger lies inside if you go in. Even better, shut the door behind you, as this means you will be able to catch if anyone is trying to take you by surprise! When you are inside a room, you have the benefit of finding a favorable spot and shoot your enemy from there.

It is good to discover building an get loot, however, in doing so, never forget to move carefully and look around the corner whenever you can for any signs of the enemy. The best way to learn this is to practice a few wild deaths and eventually, you will learn to take things more sensibly!

Crouch Whenever Possible

Always duck down when you are out moving in the open. It will have less recoil on your weapons and will make less noise as compared to when you are walking. You can hide and move at the same time. Crawling can help increase your chances of survival.

Upgrade Weapons into Higher Rarity Versions

Always take the rarest weapon in any offer. The rarer a weapon the more lethal it is.

Traps Can Provide Very Easy Kills

If an area has more enemies use traps to your advantage. You can place traps in entrances to a house, back entries, or anyplace appealing for players to rush in for loot. Traps may not kill your enemy, but it will hurt them enough and make them an easy kill for later.

Choose Your Fights Carefully

If you don't have good aims, weapons or resources. Our advice, don't get into a combat unless you have no other choice. If you are not confident, don't take any aggressive actions. Never fire from a distance unless you are sure you can chop the head off. Missing the shot will risk in exposing your location and might put you in danger.

Don't Wait to Use a Shield Potion

Shield potions are no doubt important, however, consuming them can take some time and also expose you towards the risk. A single drop can get your shield boosted up to 50%. However, these don't help against any injury that you may have. You can smear up to two of these potions if you're blessed enough to bag a pair, that is.

A Good Defense is a Good Offense

Since the last man surviving is the winner of the match. Don't stress over counting how many have you killed. Keep your gaming strategy more passive and avoid combat as much as possible. Your defense should be as good as your offense. The only battles that matter most are the player who is between you and your streak. Let the rest of the players fight among themselves.

Surviving The End-Game

You are now among the top few players and you have positioned yourself well by fortifying. Unfortunately, no matter how strong a shelter is, it's destructible. Since you are almost near to the victory, it is important to not just rely on one strategy but have a plan A or B. Always try to predict the next move of your enemy and identify what move you will play next also how you can best use the map to your advantage.

Duo and Squad Mode Tips

Here are few important strategies to adapt when playing in team or duo.

Landing

It is of imperative importance to communicate your landing location. Specify the structure and either the whole team should go to the same location or you can divide to get most of the resources.

If you and your team has landed in the same spot, highlight the amount and type of goods each player will take so neither has too many or too less. If you encounter any enemy call for back-up immediately. It's important that you act and respond quickly when cracking open chests or responding to a teammate's appeal for help.

Fighting

If you get caught in any danger or if you get any surprise guest, immediately inform your team. Think of, communication as oxygen for survival in duo or team. However, don't mix communication with over-information. Don't write an easy on where your enemy is located at. Keep it simple to avoid any misunderstandings. Keep it natural, check the compass and see what path is heading? Anything of interest?

When you're in the match, it's a good idea to try and bring down the same adversary. Always highlight which enemy or structure you are aiming at.

Building

Don't forget to gather as many resources as you can. Whether its chopping trees or looting from fallen adversaries. Keep in contact with your squad when you are building to ensure battle monogamy. If you both have got ample resources, building amazing structures is just a child's game. However, it also means that you have to keep checking on your partner to ensure he is as full as you or in case they may need back-up.

BONUS

Best Video Channels, That Can Help You to Upgrade Your Skills

Youtubers:	Twitch:
• Ninja • Muselk • TSM_Myth • Ali-A • Dakotaz • Vikkstar123 • Cizzorz • Avxry • CDNThe3rd • BCC Trolling • TBNRfrags	• Ninja • Myth • Dakotaz • Mitch Jones • summit1g • DrLupo • Lirik • CDNthe3rd • UberHaxorNova • GoldGlove

Fortnite Glossary (Slang)

Given below is a list of slangs that are likely to be used throughout the game when communicating with other players etc. Although they are not all at least it will get you familiar.

Bush Campers

This tactic is common for a seasonal player but for a newbie this is new. Bush campers or bush camping word is used for players who hide or duck in a bush. Bush is not a defensive but more of a hiding thing. It is very hard to spot players hiding in a bush even from an average distance.

Knock(ed)

Knocking an enemy means to beat a player without killing it. Telling your squad that you have knocked an enemy, hints them that the enemy is not yet dead and he may have his allies nearby.

Launching

Launching is term referred to players who use a launchpad. You can tell your colleagues that a rival has launched so they get alert and look at the sky.

Mats

Mats is a jargon for materials, which clearly refers to wood, brick, and metal in the gameplay. Your team members may ask you to share your mats or may also say, "how are you on mats?" which is often a reference to wood, brick(stone), and metal levels.

Minis

A "mini" is more frequently a slang word used for mini-shields. To make a maximum of 50% of their shield, players need to consume at least 2 mini-shields.

One-Shot

The slang is self-explanatory.

Shield Pop

The phrase "shield pop" is used when you want to tell your colleague that you have smashed an enemy shield either partially or fully. This will give them a signal that the enemy is weak, and they can take action against it. When you bring down an enemy and notice it shield is full, this is also a good indication that the enemy might also have some good weapons.

Storm Troopers

"Storm Troopers" is the name used for enemies you are either in or out of the storm.

The Bubble

The bubble is referred to as the eye of the storm. Players may order their team-mates to start "moving toward the bubble", or "let's shape in the last/final bubble".

Heals

If a group-member ask, "do you have any heals?" they want to know if you have any medicines, which usually means health points, not shields. Heal means bandages, med-kits, chug-jugs, campfires or slurp potions. Sharing it can help you achieve your goal.

Useful Links

https://fortnitetracker.com/ - Check your Stats and Leaderboards ranking for Fortnite.

www.fortnitechests.info/ - interactive map with all chest spawn locations.

http://www.ign.com/maps/fortnite/battle-royale-hi-res/ - another interactive map for Fortnite with locations, and descriptions for items.

https://www.usgamer.net/articles/the-10-best-fortnite-battle-royale-skins/ - Top 10 Fortnite skins.

https://www.facebook.com/fortnitememes/ - Fortnite Memes =)

https://fortnite.gamepedia.com/Battle_Royale/ - Fortnite Wiki.

A note from Author

Thank You so much for reading

Fortnite Battle Royale Guide

If you enjoyed it, please take a moment to

leave a review at your favorite online retailer

such as Amazon.

Made in the USA
Middletown, DE
26 September 2018